LOVE LETTERS TO MY

Queen

Bride

BETH C. WALKER

WestBow
PRESS
A DIVISION OF THOMAS NELSON

Copyright © 2012 Beth C. Walker

Author's Website: www.queenbride.com & www.bethcwalker.com
Cover Design: Hyliian Graphics/Elizabeth E. Little http://hyliian.deviantart.com/
Interior Formatting: Ellen C. Maze www.ellencmaze.com, The Author's Mentor
Filigree Elements art credit: http://kissncontrol.deviantart.com/
Purchase additional copies of this book at www.queenbride.com or www.bethcwalker.com

All rights reserved. No part of this book may be used or reproduced by any means, graphic, electronic, or mechanical, including photocopying, recording, taping or by any information storage retrieval system without the written permission of the publisher except in the case of brief quotations embodied in critical articles and reviews.

WestBow Press books may be ordered through booksellers or by contacting:

WestBow Press
A Division of Thomas Nelson
1663 Liberty Drive
Bloomington, IN 47403
www.westbowpress.com
1-(866) 928-1240

Because of the dynamic nature of the Internet, any web addresses or links contained in this book may have changed since publication and may no longer be valid. The views expressed in this work are solely those of the author and do not necessarily reflect the views of the publisher, and the publisher hereby disclaims any responsibility for them.

Any people depicted in stock imagery provided by Thinkstock are models, and such images are being used for illustrative purposes only.

Certain stock imagery © Thinkstock.

ISBN: 978-1-4497-3209-7 (sc)
ISBN: 978-1-4497-3210-3 (hc)
ISBN: 978-1-4497-3208-0 (e)

Library of Congress Control Number: 2011960688

Printed in the United States of America

WestBow Press rev. date: 05/07/2012

Dedication

This book is dedicated to you the reader, with the prayer that you be fully blessed in every way, totally protected from all evil and harm, and completely controlled by God, Jesus, and the Holy Spirit.

To God be the glory for my loving and supportive husband Ben and family: Scott and April Cawthon, Ben and Susie Walker, Bart and Forrest Turner. To God be the glory for my grandchildren: Melanie Beth and Sarah Cawthon, Anne McKinley and Gracie Walker, and Lilly, June, and Walker Turner. This book is written with a special dedication to all of you.

To God be the glory for my awesome parents, extended family, sisters, friends, including my Wednesday worship group who have loved and supported me unconditionally. I thank God for all of you who have let Him be and do through you.

I thank you Lord for using me to write this book to bless your Royal Queen Brides. To you Lord be all the glory.

Beth C. Walker

Introduction

My prayer is that you, Christ's Queen Bride, will comprehend to the fullest how loved you are by God, Jesus above and the Holy Spirit in you and in others. It is only through experiencing this love that we are able to respond to Him in obedience.

Through my own intimacy with God I have learned that we can become whole by knowing our true identity. I have also learned that we are cherished beloved royal children of God and King Jesus' adored Queen Bride (Isaiah 54:5). God is the King of the universe so His child would be either a prince or a princess, with all the rights and privileges of a royal child. The Bible says the church is the Bride of Christ. It also says each Christian is a temple (church) where the Holy Spirit resides. Therefore each Christian surrendered to the Holy Spirit; living inside them, is Christ the King's Queen Bride. Because of that we have all the rights and privileges of this relationship. God Himself, the Holy Spirit, lives within us 24/7 and will never ever leave us. We are fully equipped and totally secure in His love!

The last chapter, Thank you Lord, is a worship guide that you can pray in response to each reading from the other chapters.

Precious Lord, bless this one worshiping you abundantly in every way in Jesus name.

Love in Him,

Beth C. Walker

Contents

Love for my Beloved	1
Comfort for my Beloved	25
Healing for my Beloved	45
Direction for my Beloved	93
Thank You, Lord	125

Love

FOR MY BELOVED

My Precious Queen Bride,

You were created in My image. I am super, the perfect guide, source of all energy, outstanding, excellent, great, good, beautiful, smart, divine, marvelous, kind, gentle, strong, winner of winners, spectacular, miraculous, precious, magnificent, terrific, responsible, all wise, exciting, perfect listener, all caring, ultimate joy giver, all comforting, full of peace, wonderful, a true treasure, perfect, awesome, totally correct, giver of laughter, healer, perfect friend, perfect spouse, perfect parent, giver of song and music, worthy of ultimate respect, totally loveable, perfect lover, the very best, and the one who has everything figured out. I have told you that I am the Vine and you are a branch of the Vine. You are part of Me! I live in you through My Holy Spirit. I will never ever leave you. You have nothing but a win-win situation every moment of your life!

Your Precious Savior,

God

LOVE LETTERS TO MY QUEEN BRIDE

My Precious One,

Come here and let Me love you. Let Me hold you a while. Rest in My arms. Rest with Me. Put your head on My breast. Relax. Feel Me encircling you and enmeshing you into Myself. I am all good. You are completely safe with me. You can fully unload with Me. I am here to take your cares away. Trust, rest, and lean on Me. I love loving you this way. I love how you listen to Me and trust Me. You have nothing to fear. You are safe with Me. You don't have to have anyone's approval. You don't have to perform for Me. I love you just like you are.

You have nothing to lose and nothing to fear. You are perfectly safe and secure with Me. I am total love and you are enveloped in Me.

I am a perfect gentleman. I live in you through My Holy Spirit. You will know when to speak and when to be silent. You will give to those who are thirsty and famished. They will drink My living water which will flow from you. Those who are not thirsty, you will love, but you will gravitate to those who hold out their cup to be filled.

I will keep you filled to overflowing because you know Me and you love Me. I can trust you with My deepest secrets because of your heart and your personal thirst for Me.

Your heart is pure. You have renounced all evil spirits and surrendered to Me. You are free of all unclean spirits. You are clean. You wash yourself with My Word and you are covered in My blood. Your lips are filled with My praises. Your ears are tuned constantly to hear Me. Well done, My good and faithful Bride. You will stay with Me in My house of love, joy, and peace forever. Precious, you are precious in My sight, My beloved.

My Very Precious One,

Today, I would like to remind you who I am and who I am in you. I am **Jehovah-Shammah**. I am always present in you. I am always with you. I am your worship center, teaching center, and praise center. I am **Jehovah-Shalom**. That means I am your peace and comfort. I am your wholeness and harmony with handling life. I am The One who gives you contentment. I am **Jehovah-Rohi**, your shepherd. I feed, lead, protect, care for, direct and guide you. I am **Jehovah-Jireh**, your provider. I give you freedom from the curse of the law of sin and death. I am the provider for all your spiritual, relational, emotional, physical, and financial needs. I am **Jehovah- Nissi**, your victor, captain, banner over all principalities and powers. I announce to all principalities and powers that My banner is over you, and Satan had no authority over you to harm you in any way. I am **Jehovah-Tsidkenu**, your righteousness. I make you righteous by allowing My son to die for your sins on the cross.

I am **Jehovah Rapha**, your healer. Your healing has been purchased for you by My son on the cross (Isaiah 53:4). I am **Jehovah- M'Kaddesh**, your sanctifier. I offer you constant forgiveness keeping you clean, pure, and holy.

I am your all in all. I am everything you could want, need or desire. Because you have Me, you have everything! I love you deeply, completely, and unconditionally. I find you fully acceptable, pleasing, and I totally approve of you and My Spirit within you. Wake in joy, sleep in peace, live in My abundant life! Know that I am the best spouse, father, friend, and church you will ever have! I am always with and in you!

You are My Beloved. Let Me kiss your eyes, ears, and nose. You are absolutely delightful. You make Me laugh, smile, shout, and cry. I cherish you! I will hold you in My arms forever and dance and leap for joy through eternity—you and Me and Me and you! I love you!

LOVE LETTERS TO MY QUEEN BRIDE

My Precious One,

I am your perfect church, perfect spouse, perfect family, perfect friend, and perfect parent. I will always be here for you. I am available to you 24 hours a day every day. I am and will be all that you need and all you desire. With Me nothing is lacking. I am and will be able to fill all the empty holes that you need filling. I supply and will supply you with proper covering or protection and safety that you need.

Soak in My love, be drenched in My mercy, bask in My glory. I love you. I am your all in all. Your adoration to Me is sweet in My ears. I delight in the praises that come from your lips! I leap with joy as you clap and dance in your worship! I am deeply touched as you share Me and My words with your friends. I am honored, filled with honor and respect as you identify your oneness with Me. I am in awe of the way you understand that I am the Vine and you are the branch attached to Me. You know I am enmeshed in the Father and the Father is enmeshed in Me. You understand the Holy Spirit is enmeshed in you and with you, we are all connected! Your brothers and sisters filled with My spirit are also connected. I will flow through you and them and there is and will be perfect harmony—a beautiful symphony of majestic love and life. You need not concern yourself with the working of the symphony. I am the great conductor. Keep your eyes on Me. As you keep your eyes on Me and obey Me, the music will be exquisite!

My Cherished Child,

When you are weak, you are made strong. When you don't feel My power and strength, I am still with you and in you. When you feel all alone and empty, I am with you. When you feel needy and like you have nothing to give, I am with you and in you. When you need other's strength and joy, I am still with you and in you. I designed you to feel weak and need others as well as to feel strong and confident and not to feel as dependent on others. You can be assured that with all your feelings, I am with you. I will never leave you or forsake you. I will never take My Holy Spirit from you. I am loving and forgiving. I am still in control of you in your weakness and dependence.

Sometimes you feel unsteady and don't know the way. You may have made a mistake. I forgive even if you are not sure if you made a mistake or not.

Just know we are inseparable. You can fully trust, rest, rely, and lean on Me to be all you need.

My Beautiful One,

I am the one who forgives you. I make you clean, pure, and white as snow. Simply come to Me just as you are and I'll make you instantly whole, clean, and pure. Then ask Me and I will show you those you need to forgive and those you are to ask for forgiveness.

I love you deeply, fully, completely and unconditionally. I will not fail you. I will carry you through on wings of love and mercy.

I have so wonderfully made you in My image that I can't resist you. You are made in My image and I have breathed My breath into you. You can't resist Me because My very breath in you draws you to Me and Me to you.

You are beautiful, wonderful and fabulous in every way because you have asked Me to totally forgive you and take over completely in every way. I am now consuming every element of your being—your very essence. I am fully residing in you and have permanently taken over. I love My home that I have created for myself to own, enjoy, and live in every part! I will maintain My home perfectly because after all, I am God and I do everything perfectly! I am also the Perfect Host and offer perfect hospitality while maintaining a non-fail security service for perfect safety.

My Precious One,

You are not incapacitated. You are fully equipped. You are filled with Me completely. You are fully loved, complete, and fully acceptable. You are ready for any challenge. I have programmed you to win and to be a winner. You are a winner. You will not fail. I will not let you fail. You are able. You can do all things because I live in you and will do through you what I need to accomplish. If you hear anything that would differ from this, it is from the pit of hell, from Satan himself. Do not believe his lies. He has always been a liar and he would like to deceive you. Tell him to get away in the power and authority of Jesus' name and he will go. Victory is yours!

LOVE LETTERS TO MY QUEEN BRIDE

My Precious One,

I love and adore you and I am extending lavish and extravagant devotion, affection, and tenderness to you precious one because I treasure and adore you so much! I cherish all your devotion to Me. I cherish that you desperately depend on Me for confidence and security.

I am sending you people to lavish love upon. You will be loving Me as you love—as you extravagantly, passionately, and tenderly adore them with so much affection, support, and conversation.

Never mind if they don't return this love. You can come back to Me and I will supply you with all the affection, support and conversation you need.

My darling, My delight, you are the one I cherish and adore. Don't try to figure people out and don't analyze, criticize, or judge them. Take whatever they want to give you and enjoy it, but come to Me for any lack on their part. They are not Me. Only I can fully satisfy you like you need satisfying. Only I can fully cherish, love, adore, and lavish extravagant love, conversation, tenderness, and affection on you like you need. I desire your love so much! I desire you because I created you. Yes, I desire your love like you desire Me. Yes, my love, I adore you! Sometimes you are so busy that you don't listen to Me. I want to hold you in my arms, kiss you with ten thousand kisses and tell you how enraptured I am with you.

It bothers Me when you get too busy with other things and can't hear Me. I want you to talk to Me and let Me talk to you throughout the day. I love to tell you how I adore you and your adoration to Me. I love to move and speak through you. I love you!

LOVE LETTERS TO MY QUEEN BRIDE

My Love, My Sweetheart, My Precious One,

I love you! I love you! You are exquisite, fabulous, adorable, and I am absolutely delighted that you are My wonderful, awesome Queen Bride who is hooked to My side. I know how you are forever dependent and needy for Me. I am delighted with your "clinginess" that you call it. I am not like the others who would say "get away— I've had enough of you—quit being so dependent and needy." I love it! I love how you constantly want Me to talk to you and you to Me. I love it! You are great! You are awesome! You are totally saturated with Me. I love you so much! When I see you, I see Myself in you. You have partaken of all of Me, and I feel Me in you. My sweetheart, My Bride, My wonderful creation, I created you to love Me and you have chosen to be consumed with Me, and have Me with you. I love our fellowship and conversations. I love your affection and My lavishing you with My deep, deep ravishing love.

I have your full attention and you have Mine. We are dripping with love for each other.

I love you the way you love Me! I love the way you love Me, and oh My love, how I am so deeply in love with you! You are My refreshment. I am yours. In Me you live and breathe. You know how I love to drench this affection on you. You savor each moment as I savor our special moments together.

You are the grass and I am the rain. You are the bird and I am your sky. You are the branch and I am the tree. You are the fish, and I am the water. We move in glorious harmony in the Holy Spirit's fabulous melody.

My love, we can dance through eternity in this love song. You have learned to pull away from the world and to dance with Me in our love song that we will dance together throughout eternity.

Let Me kiss you on your face, your nose, your ears, and your eyes. Let Me kiss you with a thousand kisses. You drink, like a dying man in a desert, all of My love. I love you. I love you. I love you. I adore and cherish you!

Awesome is the word I use to describe how truly exquisite I think you are. My Holy Spirit in you will never ever fail. He will always lead you into all truth. You can be fully confident of Me in you.

Don't ever doubt Me or My Holy Spirit in you. I love Me in you. Even if you doubt Me, I will love you. I will kiss you with My thousand kisses. I will affirm and edify you. I will never criticize, put you down, or hurt your feelings. I will always shower love and affection all over you.

My love, I know how much you love Me and need Me. I will help you even to be confident of Me in you. I will show you how to handle each situation.

Let Me rock you in My arms. Yes, let Me just hold you. It's going to be alright. Everything is going to be okay. You are precious, precious, priceless, priceless, and precious. Please don't forget how I feel about you.

Remember when you are weak, I am made strong. I love your weakness. I am not like the world. I will never be like the world. I will never say to pull yourself up by your bootstraps. I will always do your pulling and bidding.

The battle is never yours, but Mine. Always remember: come to Me with all your labor and heavy burdens, and I will give you rest.

My Precious One,

When you are in My Kingdom, you will have to make some decisions. There will be those who will criticize you. Don't worry. You have Me, and I will support and love you. I will hold and nurture you. Sometimes you doubt the decisions you make. Don't worry. Give Me your doubt. I will take care of everything.

Now, let Me tell you how precious you are—precious, precious, beautiful, awesome, WOW! Let Me kiss you again with My one thousand kisses. You always love My thousand kisses! You are altogether beautiful in My Robes of Righteousness. You look absolutely splendid in your royal attire. You glow with The Presence of My Spirit. The aroma that you radiate is sweeter than the sweetest rose. I love you. I love you! How beautiful you are My Love, how beautiful you are. How I love to lavish all My gifts on you and through you. I bless you. I am so proud of you.

Come to Me when you are weary and are wiped out. My love, give Me your weariness and your burdens. Trust, rest, rely and lean on Me. Let Me fill your love tank.

My precious, you are so precious. Everything about you is precious. You have been exquisitely shaped and molded by the most expert artist. There is not one flaw in you. When I look at you, I see My precious blood covering you from head to toe totally cleansed from all unrighteousness. You are clean because of My finished work on the cross. I would do it all over again just for you if that were necessary. I love you!

My Precious One,

I know your willingness to wash My feet with your tears and with your joy. I will be faithful and true to you, not just because of your love and devotion, but because I am fully devoted to you. I would die a thousand deaths again just for you because My love for you is that powerful. I will treat you tenderly and will be your strong man.

Look around at My children. I have given you brothers and sisters that love Me as you do. They love Me with the same devotion as you and they will hold your faint arms up. They will hold you and love you tenderly. You will feel My love through them.

I want you to rest as a baby in the womb. Float around secure, safe, undisturbed, and free of all care—free of any thinking. See angels even guarding you in the womb.

LOVE LETTERS TO MY QUEEN BRIDE

My Precious One,

I love your neediness of My love. I see and feel you are longing to be nurtured, loved, strengthened, affirmed, edified, encouraged and comforted. You are not unreasonable, silly, spoiled, or immature. I love to meet your deep needs. I think you are awesome! My Queen, it delights Me that you come to Me, and I want to put you on My royal pedestal and do that for you. I feel your passion for Me, and I want you to feel My passion for you! Please don't be troubled by all of those in the world who are so uncaring, who do not want to join in our parties and celebrations, and those who don't want to join in our dance of love. Let them go. You have Me and I am The King of the love dance. I want you beside Me feeling My passion for you. I can give you all and do all for you. Don't be needy for them first. Give your whole heart to Me.

It is so fun to sing, dance, laugh, and love with you. I love your conversation. I love to hug and be hugged by you. I love when you empty yourself out to Me and when you are vulnerable with Me. It shows Me that you trust Me totally. My dear, dear, precious, beautiful, and awesome one in whom My Spirit lives, I love pouring Myself into every crevice of your priceless self. I love your coming to Me empty and helpless so I can blow My holy kisses of anointing to fill and soothe you. I love to tell you over and over and over how much I cherish and adore you. I want to tell you over and over again how proud I am of you because you let Me do for you. You are not caught up trying to do this or that, but caught up in just loving Me and letting Me love you. This pleases Me the most. You don't have to try to figure out anything. I will figure out and do everything for you and through you. Please rest in Me and rest in My love. Delight in My compassion, mercy, and grace.

I know you love loving My other children. That is another beautiful thing about you. I love the way you let My Spirit do this through you. You will never become empty giving with My Spirit operating through you, as long as you are letting Me do it through you.

I treasure your coming to Me for your friend's needs. You can come to Me anytime to discuss your passion for My Kingdom work and those you cherish and who are so precious to you. I'm not too busy or distracted. I am here every second, 24 hours a day. I love your conversation. My conversations with you are exciting and stimulating. I love our bonding and intimacy.

Stop feeling guilty about anything. I forgive you instantly when you repent. I am not a critical, condemning, controlling lover. Come to Me with the slightest feeling of guilt and give it to Me. I will forgive, love and affirm you. Whatever is bothering you, we will talk about it and I will show you the way. I will always empower you to go the right way and you will feel peace and joy going in the way that I point you.

You have nothing to fear. You are clothed in royal clothes. Your clothing is stamped in the most precious and brilliant jewels of My Most Royal Righteousness purchased for you at Calvary. Everywhere you go you wear My Royal Robe. You are clothed beautifully in your robe. You are crowned with My Royal Crown of Righteousness. Your crown sparkles and is dazzling with the brilliance of My righteousness. Remember who you are, My Queen, everywhere you go. Remember who lives inside you—My Holy Spirit. Remember whose arms you will run back into at the end of your day to be saturated with My passionate love, kisses, hugs of affection, and compassion.

My sweetheart, don't trouble yourself with those who are disinterested, unkind, and even cruel to you. Don't let them rob you of our sweet fellowship, joy, and peace. You and I—we are bonded together—we are one. We are a couple who are passionately in love with each other. You waste time that you could enjoy by being bothered by them. My love, you can pray for them. They don't know how much I love them and how much joy and happiness I could give them. Yes, Love, I have heard your prayers for them and I am doing everything I can to draw them into our love song. They are created with a free will so even though I am doing all, I still have to let them choose to come with us. Now, let go. Turn your thoughts to Me, to us, to our love song.

I love you! I love you! I love you!

My Precious, Precious, Precious, One,

Only I can love you like you need to be loved. Rest as a little baby on My shoulder. Let Me rock and soothe you. Let Me pat you gently until you feel safe, secure, and loved.

I am never too busy for you. I am always interested in talking to you and for you to talk to Me. You are extremely important to Me. There is never anything or anyone who is more important to Me than you. I am always ready to stop, to listen, and talk. I delight in communion with you.

I will never neglect you. You are the one I cherish, treasure, and adore! I want to lavish you with loving care and attention. I am always planning ahead to make sure you are cared for in a well thought out extravagant way. You are so important to Me. Look to Me for all the love you need. I will meet your every need and fill all the empty holes in your heart. You are My delight, My prize, My sparkling jewel. Words can't describe My love and devotion to you. I want to and will do My best for you in every way. I know what your needs and desires are even better than you know, and I will be extremely attentive to making sure they are all taken care of in the perfect time. I am never too late, but always there at the perfect time to take care of and provide for you. Look not to others but to Me to be your complete source of fulfillment. They can't and you will only be disappointed if you are expecting them to totally fulfill you.

The whole world belongs to Me and everything in it. You are My Queen, My Bride. I want you to rest in My love and rest in My provision for you. I will always keep My Queen, My Bride satisfied because I am a kind and generous King.

Because I will keep you lavishly loved, fulfilled, and satisfied, you will be able to lavishly love others unconditionally. There is nothing I want you to do for Me. I will do everything through you. You will be so loved that love will flow out of you. I will continuously pour into your cup so that it will spill over to others.

Rest My Bride, My Queen, in My love. Rest, relax, and enjoy Me as I enjoy you. I am your Husband who thinks you are awesome. I love you so much!

Comfort

FOR MY BELOVED

COMFORT FOR MY BELOVED

My Precious One,

I love that you choose to spend this time with Me—to completely stop what you are doing to be with Me. You are My joy and delight! I know that you are fully devoted to Me. Let Me hold you close. Put your head on My chest. Feel My heartbeat. I love you passionately and unconditionally. You don't have to perform or do anything for Me. All I want is your love and devotion—for you to release and surrender your all in My arms of love. I will do everything through you. I will even think and feel for you. My Spirit in you will do this. Rest with Me. You can go limp in My embrace. You can fully let go, to be still and quiet. Trust—you want someone to fully trust with your feelings, emotions, hurts, disappointments, and even where you think you have failed. You can trust Me.

I will never criticize or love you less no matter where you are, how you feel, or what you have done. I cherish you! I am devoted to you! You are My Bride, My wife, My Queen. We are bonded together and are one. I will go with you everywhere. I will never leave you alone or abandon you. I will prop you up if you are about to faint. I will always be your underlying support. I will hold you in my arms tenderly when you just need to be held and loved.

You have nothing to fear or worry about. If I can part the Red Sea, shut the lion's mouth, save Noah and his family, know I can take care of all your concerns. Come to Me, my precious one with your heavy burdens and I will give you rest, for My yoke fits easy (A Royal Crown) and My burdens (they aren't yours to carry) are light.

My Precious One,

I am so much more powerful than some wimp spirit. I am God— The Lion who roars—The Lion of Judah. I am never in defeat. I am never intimidated. I never ever fail. I live in you!

Don't let yucky, wimpy, sleazy, garbage, stale, stinky, creepy, spirits depress you. They are nauseating bugs. Let My Living Water of Love pour all through you, in you, over you and then let it run off of you. My Living Water flowing through and out of you will clean out the bugs. It will flush the bugs out. Let My Living Water of Love pour through you continuously. You have all of Me all the time, pouring through you all the time. The bugs don't have a chance. They have to go. I am The Holy Spirit, The Living Water in you. I am the Living Word in you. I inhabit you.

You have nothing to fear. Stay close to Me. Stay under my robes of love. Stay very close. I will instruct you. I will love you. I will enclose you in love—My love—complete love at all times. You have nothing to fear. I am love and I live in you. I will help you. I will help you. You have Me. You have Me in you and with you, and I am looking out for you. Just let My Living Water flow through you. Don't focus on anything but Me. You will be staying tight with Me. I am The River of Living Water that will keep you clean and those around you.

I am the purifier. I am joy, light, and love. I live in you and will be with you. I love you.

In this world there will be tribulation, pain, and suffering, but linked to Me we will go through. I want you to stay with Me. I am The River. I am The Purifier. I am your life.

My Precious Child,

I am your strong tower, your resting place in the storm. Come to Me with all your labor and heavy burdens and I will give you rest. Yes, even with the upheaval and unrest, you can find a quiet, serene, loving place with Me. You must come to Me and let Me quiet your fears and discontent. Only in Me can you find complete rest and contentment. Do not move until you are content, rested, comforted, quiet, and have ceased all striving. I have not called you to change your loved ones, your church, yourself, your friends, or the world. Only I can change you and them. I have called you to surrender to Me so that I through you can build up My Kingdom here on earth. Yes, I have called you to pull down strongholds and to be a warrior, but you do it through love. My major weapon of warfare is love. Love's arms are praise, worship, and the gifts of the Spirit. You will do major damage in the enemy's territory as you love and allow Me to minister spiritual gifts through you. Come to Me. Stay with Me. At the slightest discontentment, let Me quiet you. The more rested and content you are, the better I am able to move through you.

There will always be war and rumors of war. Satan will leave you alone for periods of time, but he will always be around on earth until I destroy him in the lake of fire. But rejoice, for I have overcome the world, and I have set My kingdom of heaven on earth. Yes, the kingdom of God is at hand. Yes, the kingdom of God is in you and in your midst. You must tap into it in the midst of the turmoil and discontent raging all around you.

You tap into My kingdom by laying aside your own agenda, plans, and control of your life. Stay in praise throughout the day. You can read Isaiah and John. You can allow yourself to become quiet and content before Me so that I can talk to you in your prayer time with Me. I can hear you all the time when you talk to Me, but you can't hear Me when you are so discontented. You tap into My kingdom when you pray for your enemies and your country's enemies. You wrestle not against flesh and blood, but Satan and all his demons. You cannot be content until you forgive and love. I can't minister My gifts correctly through you until you love, forgive and pray for those who neglect and persecute you. Pray that they will be released from Satan's grip and be filled with My Spirit.

I have given you John 14:20-21 and Matthew 28:18-20. I have given you a vision, focus, and a purpose. These can only be carried out as you let go of the control in your life and let Me love you and love through you. Remember when you are weak, I can be strong in you.

My Precious One,

You are so special to Me—so dear to My heart. You are "the apple of My eye!" I adore you! (Psalm 17:18)

Let Me hold you in My arms. You can rest here above the cares of the world. You can be secure, safe, and thoroughly loved. There is nothing you must do for Me to get My approval. You are complete just as you are.

I will be with you today and be your best friend. You can talk to Me and we can be tight together. I won't leave you, scold you, criticize or judge you. I am here only to love you.

Please stay close to Me. I love you loving Me. I love loving you!

You're so easy, easy to love. Don't be needy or worry about others who don't approve or need your love. You have Me. I am enough. I am so much more than enough. I am The One who can and will supply all your emotional, physical, material, relational, spiritual, and financial needs. Rest in Me your total need provider.

LOVE LETTERS TO MY QUEEN BRIDE

My Precious One,

I am the Alpha and Omega—the Beginning and the End. I am never too old, too young, too early, or too late. Because I live in you, you are never too old, too young, too early, or too late. My Spirit in you is always just right—perfect. I am perfect in you—Perfect! As you give me full control and you fully surrender, I take over perfectly. I am perfect and I do not even make mistakes. I am fully devoted to you to watch over and care for you. All you have to do is trust Me and believe. Your only requirement is to trust, surrender, and believe. Then, My treasure, I will do it all—all through you. Don't even worry about trusting, surrendering, and believing because I will help you do that also. I am all wise and I hold the keys to the kingdom. I will unlock all doors for you! Just enjoy Me as I enjoy you! Believe My love. Bask in My glow!

Your trusting, surrendering, and believing will come as you spend time with Me, listening to Me, reading My love letters to you and letting Me love on you. You are fabulous, beautiful, awesome, adorable and made in My image! I am enraptured with you!

My Precious One,

I know your needs. Thank you for coming to Me. I am working on your behalf all the time. Keep your faith in Me. If you saw how it was going to happen, then it wouldn't be faith. I will even supply you with faith. I will supply you with love, joy, peace, and patience.

I want you to enjoy Me at all times as I enjoy you. Come to Me often to talk to Me and let Me talk to you.

I am never too tired or bored with you. I find you interesting and exciting. Stay close to Me. Always stay close to Me. I won't fail you. I will help you. Even the things in the past that trouble you, I am fully taking care of.

I will help you and you will be strong, confident, and ready for any challenge. I will keep you comforted, stimulated, motivated, and on track. I will always cause you to be a victor and never a victim. I have made you mine. I am hooked to your side. We are one in My Spirit.

My Holy Spirit in you gives you My wisdom. You are fully equipped with My wisdom that you can use all the time. Take much time to be alone with Me. Study My word. Enjoy your worship and I will tell you everything you need to know.

LOVE LETTERS TO MY QUEEN BRIDE

My Precious One,

People, places, things, power, riches, etc. will never fully satisfy. Only I can fill you up completely. Drink all of Me. Be consumed with Me. Be intoxicated with Me. I am your place of joy, contentment, warmth, safety, security, comfort, and satisfaction. I fully approve of you. I am delighted with you! You bring Me great joy. My Spirit in you gives you keen discernment. You choose Me first. You make the right choices. Even when you don't, I am delighted with you. I know that eventually you will come around to being fully satisfied with Me and making the right choices. My love is unconditional. My forgiveness is never exhaustible.

Your safe and cozy place is with Me. I am your all in all. I meet all your needs. I make no mistakes. I have all your affairs in order. I hear and understand all your concerns. There is nothing too difficult for Me. I am always on time and I never make mistakes. I am the King of Kings and Lord of Lords. I am all wise and all knowing. I live in you. The same authority that I rule and reign with is yours because I give you My Holy Spirit. I have all the power of the universe. I am the number one power and authority. You have the same power because of My Holy Spirit in you.

What is power? It is love. I am Love. What is authority? It is love.

COMFORT FOR MY BELOVED

My Precious One,

I am with you and in you. I will not let your foot slip. I will not let you fail. Relax. I am in control. You don't have to figure everything out. You are not responsible for the work I have put you in or the job I have assigned you. You are not even responsible for carrying out the plans, goals, and vision that I have laid before you for yourself, your family, friends, and the world.

You are not responsible for the anointing or the glory to fall on yourself or others. I am asking you to just surrender to Me constantly so I can do this through you. Relax and let go. As you let go of all control, I can work through you to accomplish what I have in mind for you, your family, your friends, and the world. Come to Me daily to sit quietly at My feet to listen. Make your requests, enjoy My word, and then get very still and very quiet. Then I can speak to you the instructions I have for you and consume you with My love.

Just as I love daily, hourly to hear your praise, and feel your adoration, you need Me to affirm you and love you constantly.

I love you deeply. I love how you wait on Me. I love how you adore Me. I love how you make Me #1 in your life. I will do powerful and mighty things through you because you wait, listen, and obey Me.

My Adored Child,

I will be with you and in you. I will be delighted with Me in you today—we are one. I know you will fully yield to Me because I know how much you love Me and you know I love you. You know you are safe with Me, and I am there to aid and minister to you. I will use you in a great way. You will be delighted. Your cup will spill over with joy as you are about our business. Don't be afraid, Love. I will be loving through you. I am Love and I live in you. I will never ever leave you!

Continue to soak yourself in My word and worship so you can be saturated with My comforting assuring voice. You will "feel" Me in you as you praise and worship Me because I inhabit the praises of My people.

My Precious One,

My child, come to Me. Trust Me. You can rest if you trust Me. You won't fret it you trust Me. You can't trust Me if you don't know Me. You can't know Me if you don't spend time with Me.

Come to Me. Not just to My word but to Me. I will speak to you. You have listened and studied well. I will tell you where to go and what to do. You are full and ready. I will give you words to speak to those who are needy. I have trained you well. You will give them what they need.

I am a big God so I have big vision. Don't limit Me. Don't limit what I can do through you. I want you to feel comfortable with Me but you can't be comfortable with Me if you do all the talking. I love your worship of Me and your reading of My word. I love the way you love and do for those around you. But My child, I want you to sit with Me and **let Me talk to you**. Sometimes you are anxious and afraid of what I might tell you. Sometimes you don't trust that I can take care of all your concerns. You don't have to be anxious and afraid because I only have what is good for you and those you love. I can and will take care of your concerns if you will just let go. Let go. My child, let go of the control in your life. Let Me help you. I have a longing to be your best friend. You call Me your best friend, but I really want to be your best friend.

My Spirit is in you. I won't ever leave you or forsake you. You will be successful in all that you do with you letting Me take over. You can surrender as much as you want to Me. The more you surrender, the more love, peace, joy, and success you will have. The more you surrender the larger your vision. If you notice, I didn't say the more you will do for Me. It is not as much about your doing for Me as it is about your surrendering to Me. It is about your intimacy with Me. I love you. I love you. I am for you. I am for you. Please trust Me.

You know in your head that I care deeply but I want you to know in your heart that truly I care deeply. I love you. I care for you deeply. When you have repeatedly been hurt by the world and those you love, you must take a giant leap of faith to come to Me to let Me talk to you. Jump! Take a huge leap! Jump off the cliff of worry, doubt, and fear! I am here to catch you, hold you in My arms, and kiss you with a thousand kisses. My precious ones who have been hurt the most, I desire most to kiss and heal their wounds. I want to put a warm blanket around them and roll out my royal carpet for them to dance and rejoice on.

My Precious Child,

I know you are both extremely excited and fearful at the same time at what I have called you to do. Remember that perfect love casts out all fear. I am perfect love, and I live inside you. I am also your Heavenly Father who deeply loves you and will always watch over you. I also give you the Holy Spirit—the Comforter. Not only will you comfort others, but you will be comforted. You are on a mercy mission to free the oppressed. If you become afraid or overwhelmed, focus on mercy. If you become depressed, focus on seeing the oppressed go free! Above all soak in worship and let Me speak words of love and comfort to you.

Love Me with all your heart, soul, mind and strength as I love you. Love your neighbors as yourself. Take care of yourself. Eat the correct food in the correct amounts. Get the exercise you need to keep your body healthy. Reduce all unnecessary stress in your life. Cut out your unnecessary "Martha" activities. (Luke 10:40). I must have your complete undivided attention to train you for what I have in mind for you. There is no place for a too busy "Martha" in an intense war zone. If you have listened to Me and trained well, you will be at peace even during the missions that I send you on.

You are important to your teammates. How well you listen and obey Me affects them as well as the oppressed that you will set free through My Holy Spirit abiding in you.

Again I repeat—<u>Fear not.</u> I am perfect love which casts out all fear.

You will be delighted and in awe at the rejuvenation, renewal, and replenishment that I am doing and will be doing in and through you. I will bless not only you, but multitudes that need Me. You will be blessed to the maximum on this earth and in heaven to come!

COMFORT FOR MY BELOVED

My Precious One,

I know you love your friends (as you call them "Jesus with skin on"), but always come first to Me. You will love them even more.

Don't worry about anything but trust, rest, rely, and lean on Me. Say this over and over until you are trusting, resting, relying, and leaning on Me.

I love you! I am always your adoring Daddy. I am always for you and eager to help you.

When you say help, I will fill in all the holes in your heart that the enemy shot. As I fill in every crevice I will squeeze in My comforting, healing anointing releasing My "feel good" peace, love, and joy. Just as I placed the soldier's ear back on him and the healing was instant so I touch your damaged emotions and instantly heal you.

Continue to soak yourself in My word to keep your healing. Remember that faith comes by hearing Me. Soak yourself in My words so you are saturated with My comforting assuring voice.

Precious One,

I have not given you a spirit of fear, but of love, joy, peace, and a sound mind. My Spirit is in you. The times when you feel the opposites of these that is probably not My Spirit. You will be grieved by the things that grieve My heart. Give them to Me. They are My burdens to bear. Give Me those who you are concerned for. Think of Me as being a wonderful kindergarten teacher and you and the ones you are concerned for are in My class. Come to Me and tell Me your concerns. I am The Good Teacher who would say, "Now go back and don't worry." I will take good care of that concern. I would hug you and then take care of the whole matter. If there is a part I want you to play, I will let you know. Otherwise, I would expect you to go about your normal routine. You can trust Me. I am their Savior as well as yours. *I love all My children*. I have your best interest at heart. *Trust, rest, rely and lean on Me. I love you so much.*

Healing

FOR MY BELOVED

Precious One,

I know that today you feel emotionally incapacitated to the degree that you need endless inspiration, energy, love, comfort, affirmation and affection to maintain the courage to face just this ordinary day. Tender one, precious and caring one, here I am. I delight in filling your love tank back up to overflowing. I am the Great Emancipator for the oppressed, and I am freeing you of all oppression.

You are handing Me your heart today, popped out of your chest, bleeding, broken, and bruised. You are uncovering the hideous wounds for Me to see. I see, I know, I hear, I feel. I have compassion to the limit that you cannot fathom—all for you. I am compassion. Compassion is the father of miracles. Because you have reached out to Me, you have touched My heart, and I am healing you right now. I am healing your weak, hurt, maimed, disturbed parts. I am making you whole now. I am also covering, nurturing, and protecting you. I am giving you security and assurance. I am bringing you peace, calmness, and fresh dreams. I love you deeply.

My Precious Friend,

I created you to be My friend. One reason I created you is so you could talk to Me. I want you to talk to Me without being fearful. You are My friend when you come into My presence. I want to talk to you lovingly, tenderly, and compassionately.

<u>You are My friend</u>. I want to talk to you wherever you are. I love you. The reason that I gave My life for you is so you could see Me face to face. <u>You are My friend!</u> I created you in My image so you could be My friend. I will always be your <u>very</u> <u>best</u> <u>friend</u>. You can share your deepest secrets, struggles, insecurities, pain and problems with Me. I will always have time to listen to you intently, passionately, and compassionately. You can share your desires, dreams, longings, joys, and excitement with Me. I will always have the perfect response for you! I am your <u>very best friend</u> that you can count on to be everything you need, desire and want!

When you are all alone, bleeding, hurting, needy, wounded to the core, lied to, spat upon, yelled at, treated like dirt, hated, betrayed, neglected, totally ignored, surrounded by darkness, unbelief, hopelessness, and beat up, I care. I am your friend. I understand your need and pain. When no one else is able to care or understand, I care and understand you. I feel your pain within because I am in you and with you. When those closest to you hurt you and are not able to truly be sorry to the core for their damage to you I take you in My arms and heal you to the core. I am here right now at this moment healing you. Right now I am holding you in My arms. Listen as I whisper in your ear; you are deeply loved, needed, appreciated, beautiful and wonderful. You are made in My image. I am perfect and I live in you!

I am your shelter, shield, strength, deliverer, and strong tower. I am always your help in the time of need.

My Precious One,

You are My delight. You delight in Me and I delight in you. I am with you and in you. You have found Me, The Pearl of Great Price. You have found My treasures and My joy. You allow My sunlight, My Holy Spirit to warm all places in your heart. You know that all that is good, lasting, delightful, and worthwhile is from Me. I am your purpose. I am your hobby. I am your project. You know that without Me you may as well hang it all up.

You say, "Lord, why have I not healed in this area?" I do the healing, not you. Don't look at what needs healing, but look to Me. I will take care of all your needs. I will take care of that, too. I will even help bring you through that area.

I am with you and in you. I will never leave the work I have started in you unfinished. I am completing your healing now. Trust that I am in you now. Trust that I make you whole.

My Precious One,

There is no room for criticism or judgment when you have been called to train for a mercy mission to free the oppressed. There can absolutely be no criticism or judgment of others including those I will free, yourself, or your teammates. The enemy will use this tactic first to cause a hindrance to My kingdom plans. Beware and stay in communication with Me constantly. This is essential. Offer mercy to yourself, your teammates, and those I will free. I am mercy. I am love. When you see something amiss, ask Me what your role in this is to make it right and what mine is. Ask this always with mercy and love—never with criticism and judgment. Listen to Me. I am the way.

I have created you with emotions. You may become irritated or angry with the enemy. Always remember to direct your irritation and anger toward the enemy, never the person, when you discern something is wrong. This is absolutely essential for you to remember. Keep in mind the verse, **"For we wrestle not against flesh and blood, but against principalities, against powers, against the rulers of the darkness of this world, against spiritual wickedness in high places."** *(Ephesians 6:12)* Your enemy is not you, your teammates, or the oppressed that I will use you to set free. Your enemy is Satan and his demonic forces. Rejoice because I give you victory over him!

Precious One,

When others offer you little or no light at all, it is because that is the only light they have. Don't be angry because they can't give any more. Love them. Don't harbor any resentment or self-pity.

Come to Me and I will provide you with all the light you need. I am offering you new encouragement, joy, excitement, energy, compassion, and love. I am who you need. You can share everything with Me. I want you to share all your joys, sorrows, plans, and ideas with Me. Please come to Me. Please share your life with Me. I am even interested in the trivia of your day. I care so much about you. It is because I care so much that I am so interested in you and everything about you! I love you!

Right now at this moment I am pouring so much light on you, in you, and through you that My brightness and illumination is more than enough for you and all those I bring your way.

Precious One,

I am all you need. I am enough. I am more than sufficient to richly supply all your needs, desires, wants, or wishes. Please take more of Me all the time.

No one can ever fulfill you like I can. No spouse, no friend, no angel or acquaintance will ever be able to love you as completely, passionately, abundantly, and unconditionally as I love you. No job, ministry, activity, hobby, sport, nice car, house, food, alcohol, drugs or nice things will be able to fulfill you like I can and will.

My desire for you more than any other desire is that you fully comprehend this fact to the extreme. It is not your good works and kind deeds that I desire as much as that you really know deeply, deeply consciously and unconsciously that I love you.

I want you to feel my love every moment of every day. When that happens you will cease striving, your anxiety will subside, and there will be no more self-doubt. There will be no feelings of unworthiness, defeat, loneliness, or insecurity. Your joy will be full and overflowing. You will not lack optimism. Hopelessness, depression, and weariness will be far from you.

Please give Me your "if-only" list. Yes, I know about all your "if-onlys." You say, "I could be happy if only I had this, if only this person would or would not do this, if only God would answer my prayer for this person, and if only I had more free time." My precious one, I know all and I see all. I love you and the people you are praying for more than you do. I desire the best for you and them, more than you desire it. Now, would you just please <u>believe</u> Me.

When any negative thoughts come your way, say, "I believe, Lord, You love me and them more than I do. I receive Your love and I know You have everything under control, Lord. You are so busy taking care of everything. Now I will rest in Your love. What would You have me think, say, and do next"?

My Love,

You are not alone. You have not been alone. You will not be alone. I am more real than life itself. I am more real than any person. My angels are real. They have been with you and will be with you. They are with you now. Do you remember what you read in My love letters to you in the book of John. "I am My words." Whenever you read My word, you are with Me in power. My Holy Spirit lives within you. Your enemy, Satan, would like for you to believe otherwise. A choice tool of his is to deceive you and make you feel all alone. He delights in this. He does this to hopefully make you feel sorry for yourself and rob you of joy and motivation. He, My Love, is a liar. You need to be aware of him. When he knocks on your door—don't answer. Don't even let him get a foot in your door. Pay no attention to him. Praise and worship or praying in the spirit will bore him and run him off.

Purpose—you need to remember the purpose to which you were created. You were created to be loved and to love Me—to fellowship with Me in a loving, feeling, intimate, passionate relationship. I love you! Then you are to go into the world filled with My joy, love and peace to teach others of the wonderful relationship they can have with Me so that they can have love, joy, purpose, and peace.

My precious one, study My word. Study and be equipped for every situation. My Bible is My love letter and My directions for you. My Holy Spirit will help you enjoy reading My directions. Satan will come around and try to tell you it is boring or distract you. Be aware. Ignore him or tell him to leave in My Name. He will have to go.

Another thing to be aware of when you feel alone is running to another human. Be careful who you run to. If the person will help you to get closer to Me or if the person enjoys being with Me all the time, then they are a safe person. If not, beware. You don't need anyone trying to pull your attention away from Me. I am joy, peace, and love. I give you a healthy mind and a whole self. What activities does this person choose? What does this person fill their mind with? Does this person always operate in the "fruit" of the Spirit (love, peace, joy, kindness, goodness, self-control) all the time? Do they apologize when they fail?

If one is not abiding in Me, you will not be edified, and there will not be rewarding fellowship and the nurturing and comfort that you desire. When you go to this person when you are needy, you are making yourself available for the enemy to attack. Be careful and prayerful when you are in need of company, fellowship, nurturing, affection, conversation, and edification. Always come to Me first. I know that you need humans also. Ask Me who to go to for friendship. This is very important.

HEALING FOR MY BELOVED

My Child,

Your heart aches for your own holiness and for those around you. You cry out over and over, forgive me and forgive them. You pray for yourself, you pray for others to repent and turn to the Lord.

My precious and dear one, I love you so deeply, I hear your prayers and see your efforts. It is My anointing that breaks the yoke. It is My kindness that leads to repentance.

My child, what you long for is My precious anointing for yourself and them. Come to Me. Worship Me. Offer the sacrifice of praise and worship with passion and with all your heart. When you are in grief over your own sins and theirs, dance with joy, clap your hands, shout, play your instruments, and make music in your heart. This is your declaration that says, "Lord, You reign." By making these declarations with joy, you bring My anointing. By making these positive declarations, you bring what is not into what is. You call with My power of The Holy Spirit the negative into the positive. By My Spirit you bring light into darkness. Don't wait until "you feel" like worshiping, thanking, and praising to enter in. While you are in grief, enter into worship. This brings My anointing. This breaks the yoke. The more the heaviness, the more you need to praise.

Pray to Me to prophesy. My body of believers needs encouragement. They need encouragement of who they are in Me, their gifting, and My plans and will for their life. By prophesying, they gain vision. This brings light to drive away the darkness. Again, this brings what is not into what is!

Silence is good. Wait in silence until you get a positive word. I am also with you in stillness and quietness. I love you, My child. I am with you and in you. I will never leave nor forsake you. My yoke is easy and My burden is light. Trust, rest, rely, and lean on Me totally. Fear and gloom are not of Me. Resist the latter and they will flee.

Wonderful One,

When you are feeling hurt by others, know that they hurt worse than you because Satan has blinded them. It may look like they are not in pain, but believe Me, they are. Pain is always attached to sin, maybe not at the moment, but it is part of the package. So, My precious, precious one, rest in My love. Come close to Me. Let Me feed you my words of love and comfort. If you stay with me and wait out the storm, you will be comforted in My loving arms. Don't hurry. Think of a child who comes crying to their loving parent. The child must stay there long enough to be rocked, comforted, and soothed so that their tears turn into smiles. If the child won't stay there long enough, the parent is not able to comfort and console them. So, it is with you and Me. My cherished one, always take your time with Me until you feel all your joy has returned.

LOVE LETTERS TO MY QUEEN BRIDE

My Precious One,

Your heart is precious and beautiful because I live in it. I am giving you a tender sensitivity for others who suffer from spiritual arrogance. I have sanctified the inner most part of your being. I have equipped you with the power to forgive those that don't know what they are doing. In the past you have been angry and hurt, and you will still have those moments. In the future, they will only be moments, but you will not stay stuck in self-pity and bitterness.

I have given you a great capacity to love with deep compassion. I am giving you eyes to see beneath the evil in the perpetrator. You know that the reason for their wrong choices was that they could not believe how much I loved them. They reached out for things, people, and ways to feel loved, significant, worthy, acceptable, and complete instead of reaching out to Me. I have given you My heart and My mind to understand and love them with great tenderness and compassion. I am not calling you to change them but to love them. If you love them with My love, the change is possible. There can be no trace of unforgiveness, bitterness, or self-pity for My healing power to operate through you.

If you hang on to your self-pity, unforgiveness, or bitterness you will be in the same boat as they are. You say, "Lord, it is impossible to love and forgive them. My feelings are so hurt."

Yes, my precious one, it is impossible for you, but with Me all things are possible and I live in you. As you stay attached to Me, The Vine, great and mighty miracles will be accomplished. You see, there was a time when they hurt like you hurt, but they really didn't understand that they could come to Me. Yes, they heard it preached, and they knew it in their heads, but they just were not able to really believe how much I loved them so they could turn to Me. So have My Spirit of compassion for them. Look beneath your hurt and self-pity to see how scarred, wounded and unfulfilled they must be to cause them to make wrong choices. It was My Spirit of compassion that enabled Me to go through with dying on the cross. I am giving you My Spirit of compassion. I am enough. I am all you need. Stay close to Me. Love Me and be loved! In Me you have the victory!

My Precious One,

When you are feeling "used", unloved, hurt, and angry, come to Me. Your problem is not your problem. Your problem is your view of the problem. When you are having these negative emotions, you are in the valley of looking at evil operating. Come with Me. Get in My helicopter and we will fly out of all the mess. We will fly up to the mountain of joy, love, peace, and total contentment where you will feel fulfilled, pampered, and loved. When others let you down, it is because they live in the valley. They have never been with Me on the mountains or they have forgotten they can live there with Me. Don't think about the evil in the valley. Stay with Me. Focus on Me. Listen only to Me. Remember the phrase, "Hear no evil, see no evil, speak no evil."

Add to that, "think on no evil." I inhabit the praise of my people. Pain, depression, oppression has to go as you praise. You force out all that negativity with praise! Be raised with praise!

My Precious One,

The way out of hell here on earth is to praise and worship Me. Paul knew this and while he was behind bars for preaching the gospel, he worshiped Me with all of his heart. The jail bars fell as the angels came to release him. Your problem is not your problem; it is your attitude about the problem. Your situation can be turned from hell to the kingdom of God—from total frustration to indescribable joy as you worship and praise. You are the one I love. I tell you this because I love you. I want you safe, secure, confident and loved because you are Mine. You belong to Me. I love you so much!

If you hand Me the enemy's spit that is in your face with a grateful and thankful heart, for My love, I will transform that which comes against you into holy anointed healing oil to comfort, heal, and bring great joy to you and those in your path. It will become your baptism of fire to consume you and all those around you. My precious one, no weapon formed against you shall prosper. You can and must dance in the fire. It will not burn you. The enemy can shoot from all sides, and I will increase your joy, peace, and love as you dance to My heartbeat. Lift your hands and heart to Me. Place your heart in My hands. It is safe and secure with Me.

LOVE LETTERS TO MY QUEEN BRIDE

My Precious One,

When you are treated wrongly and you or your words are not accepted, look immediately to Me and praise Me. When others are treated wrongly and they are not accepted, praise Me. This will be a survival tool for you. It will help you get through the painful moment to steady your emotions. If the person in the wrong only understood My love for them and My kingdom ways, they would gladly flow in My Spirit with love, joy, and peace.

If you are to be My disciple, you must first learn to have a heart of compassion for those who are treating you and others wrongly. You will not have the patience, so you must rely on My Spirit in you to get through difficult moments. You must constantly be in a state of praise and worship to Me and keep your mind set constantly to winning others into My kingdom. Satan would love to get you off guard so you must be on guard at every moment.

Life is like a football game. Satan and his demons are your opponents. If you only play defensively, your struggle will be greater. Listen to Me, your coach. I will give you offensive plays that will keep Satan whipped and keep you and your teammates way ahead.

Trust, rest, rely on Me solely. Never take offense when people hurt you and your loved ones, but pray that My light and love would flood their hearts. When you take offense, you let Satan score points. Keep focused on Me and My words and winning others to Me. I am the King of the Universe. My son has already defeated Satan. I laugh at his puny plans. So, precious one, keep on pointing others to Me by living a life of peace, joy, love, and praise. Let Me laugh through you so the world can see I am in control and I have already won over Satan.

LOVE LETTERS TO MY QUEEN BRIDE

My Precious One,

You don't have your eyes on Me, but on that other one. I am the only one who is able to fully love you the way you want to be loved, nurtured, and cared for. Don't look at other relationships to totally fulfill and complete you. Look to our relationship.

Absorb yourself in Me. Focus on Me. Focus on My word. Stay with Me in communication until you are released with peace and joy to make your next move.

You may admit your pain and what you would like, but don't replay it over and over in your mind. Please don't be angry with Me about your situation. If you love Me, trust Me, stay with Me. I will give you that special joy, excitement, peace, and relationship of love you long for. If you give your thoughts to Me and stay with Me you will find total contentment.

There is no gain when you complain. Watch your thoughts. Keep all your thoughts pure, holy, and blameless. I want you to soar in My abundant life.

My Cherished One,

I am so glad you are with Me, that in your neediness you come to Me. I truly love you and appreciate you. I love every fiber of you, and I approve of you. When others don't accept My words I have given you to give out, come to Me like you are doing. They didn't always accept Me and My words. Remember, in my own hometown they wanted to push Me over a cliff. I know your heart. I know that you listen and obey Me. I am very pleased with you and after all, you already know that My opinion is the one that really counts. Don't worry—be happy—rejoice because now and later exceeding great rewards are awaiting you.

You are My Sweetheart, My Bride, My Treasure! I am more real than life itself. I am more devoted to you than any person. I delight in you! You are fun, exciting, and interesting to me. You have My Spirit living in you which makes us soul mates. Your soul will one day be with Me in eternity. That isn't far away and it will be glorious! You will love heaven. Everything will be perfect there. You will be perfectly understood and you will perfectly understand everyone there.

My precious one, this challenge you face today, I will take care of perfectly. Don't worry, there will be a new challenge tomorrow. I will fully take care of that also. Just draw closer and closer to Me. Don't worry about people. Stay focused on Me, My love for you, and My will for you.

LOVE LETTERS TO MY QUEEN BRIDE

My Precious Child,

You must have compassion for all. Never make a judgment on anyone. To the degree that you have mercy and compassion will be to the degree you are shown mercy and compassion.

You don't know how the life experiences, parents, acquaintances, mentors, and friends have caused a person to act and react. It is your job to love and not judge. When you are given discernment, ask for a double portion of love. Often you are allowed to see evil so that I can minister through you effectively to them. I cannot work through you without your love.

Come to Me. Stay with Me. Get lost in praise, thanksgiving and worship. You are not able to love the unlovely on your own. As you soak in My words of love I melt, mold, and fill you to overflowing. It will be Me loving them through you. They will have an opportunity to experience My unconditional love and mercy through you. You are a walking gospel. You are My Living Bible. This is how you win them over to Me and My Kingdom of Love.

It is absolutely essential that you schedule long love soaks with Me daily and stay with Me constantly to keep yourself saturated in My love. Be aware of your thought life. Are you dwelling on Me and My love or the evil and the one the evil one is influencing? Whoever and whatever you dwell on becomes your god. I know you will choose Me! I know you will choose to be embraced in My loving arms continuously.

LOVE LETTERS TO MY QUEEN BRIDE

My Precious One,

I understand your pain and hurt. I understand your lack of hope. I understand how you feel neglected and betrayed. That is the flesh. My spirit lives in My people. They are My children. Their flesh just gets in the way. Forgive them.

Only I can love you like you need to be loved, only I. I know it is hard to get in touch with warm feelings after being hurt, but please don't stay in grief, depression, or lack of hope. There will be better days. Joy always comes in the morning. Don't be bitter, don't judge. I bring you hope. There will be more moments of love, gladness, warmth, joy, peace, and oneness with your brothers and sisters in Christ. Don't get consumed by the current disappointments.

Keep on loving. Love and forgive. I will sprinkle My warmth on you. Receive it. Receive My love. Let Me enfold you in My heart—My arms. Let Me kiss you. Let Me throw My light on you and warm you. Let Me pour My oil of healing on all those sore and rough spots. It will ease the pain and soften your sore spots.

Get past all those who don't approve of you and who hurt you. Love them with all your heart. Sweep your side of the street. Keep your heart clean. Grow beautiful fruit and flowers in the garden of your heart. Dance, sing, play and enjoy your fruit and flowers. I am in your garden. You are never alone. I am God. I will be there. Jesus, The Holy Spirit and My angels will keep you company. We will all keep you company in your garden. We like you! We love you! We won't let you down or have a mean thought about you. We won't neglect you.

Why do you stay so troubled that the others are not in your garden? Stop focusing on them. Please focus on Jesus, the Holy Spirit and Me. Enjoy others but let them go. Let go of control. Be happy with Me. Please be happy with just Me. Let Me be your lover. I am The King—your protector, provider, and lover. Please focus on Me. I will fulfill your every need. I will fill your love tank. The others can't be Me and fulfill like Me. I will go with you everywhere.

We may have to go through the jungle, but I will be there to hold your hand. There will be snakes, scorpions, alligators, lions, tigers, and some wolves dressed as lambs. I will put an invisible shield about you that they can't penetrate. You will see and know. We will go back to our little garden after the walk in the jungle and we will be refreshed again.

Keep your eyes and heart on Me. Love everyone. If they are unable to love—lean on Me. I will keep your love tank full.

I will love you. I am loving you now. I will always give you a fresh love talk. I will never quit loving you. We are one with My Spirit in you. We are an item! I will hold you and whisper love messages to you. I will shout from the rooftops, mountaintops, and billboards. I LOVE YOU!

Everywhere you go—everything you do I will be there loving you! I love you! I love you! I love you! I am for you! I am for you!

LOVE LETTERS TO MY QUEEN BRIDE

I am The Way. I am *your* Life and your *v*ery breath. You are safe in My arms. I will never leave you, forsake you, or betray you. Your interests are #1 with Me.

Don't let the wolves disguised as lambs, or the alligators distress you. You only need My 100% love.

My Precious One,

You feel heavy sometimes because the harvest is full and the laborers are few. You want to help everyone and you know you are physically limited to do so much. Sometimes you feel unhealthy, guilty for turning some away. Please accept your limitations. Please accept when I tell you so. My precious one, come to Me. I didn't intend for you to help everyone. Sometimes, I allow you to feel their burdens so you can pray for them and truly care. Stay close to Me. Sometimes I may allow you to minister and sometimes I want you to allow someone else to. Listen to the small still voice very carefully. Listen closely. Stay very close to Me. What you do for Me is very significant if you let Me do it through you and I have told you to do it.

You don't have to perform for Me. My yoke fits easy and My burdens are light. As you listen and stay close you will hear My voice and know it is Me.

Remember <u>your greatest task is to be loved and filled with Me</u>. As you are loved and as My anointing comes over you, your right hand won't know what your left hand is doing. I will be doing My work through you. Sometimes even silence speaks louder than words. My anointing on you can be so great that others will feel My presence.

I love you, My precious one. You love Me. Come to Me just as you are. Come to Me with your mistakes, doubts, fears, confusion, responsibilities, cloudiness, and whatever. Just let Me love you. Be loved. Know you are loved. Know you have My approval and that is what really matters.

My Love, My Queen, My Precious One,

My heart feels what you feel. You presented My most precious pearls and they were rejected. It is not you that is being rejected, but Me. You were on track. You were listening to Me and you were obedient to Me. You didn't miss it. You were on track and on time. This is all about Me and not about you. You even feel angry. That is okay. Just give it to Me.

My prize, My precious one, you are the apple of My eye. Don't you worry about a thing. Don't fret and be upset anymore. This is My problem. Get rid of all anger and bitterness. I will part the Red Sea.

Take your eyes off of the problem. I can handle it perfectly. I want you to be focused. Use your time and energy as I will direct you. Totally take your mind off this matter. I have much joy and delight for you.

You are My Queen, My Bride. I want My Queen seated beside Me on My throne knowing that we are one in My Spirit. I am #1. I am always right. My Holy Spirit in you is more than able to handle absolutely anything that Satan blows your way. He is a loser. Those who listen and follow him are to be pitied.

I am a gentleman. My Holy Spirit in you is also a gentleman. We never force or beg. We love. We give to those who are thirsty and who are ready to receive. Some are very thirsty and some just a little bit.

Again, I tell you, I have a solution that won't rob your delight and joy. The babies in My kingdom are as wonderful as My most mature warriors. I will give them all what they need and what they can handle.

Don't get focused on a few fish. I have millions of ponds and fish that I am concerned about. My Spirit in you causes you to be an awesome fisherman in My Kingdom. Move on. Get ready for your next assignment. I love you. I am your daddy. Now go, relax and rest from your fishing.

Dear Precious One,

I love you. I know with all the disappointments down here it is hard for you to comprehend that sometimes. I am not like all the rest. I know your desire to be filled with Me and My anointing. Come close to Me. Spend time with Me and I will fill you up.

All your concerns and disappointments—place them all in My hands. I have not forgotten you. Press in to Me. Press into My presence. You will find Me. Only in Me will you find total fulfillment. I know about your requests. You don't have to beg Me. Press into Me. Come close. Don't get in a hassle about anything.

I am The Way, The Truth, and The Life. Stay close to Me. Stay in worship. Stay in prayer. Stay in My word. You will see. You will know. The Way will unfold.

You look for the plan. I am The Plan. My ways are simple and easy. Stay with Me. My yoke fits easy and My burdens are light. I am not uncaring or unconcerned about anything. I want intimacy with you. I want you to be in love with Me at all times, even when it seems as if My answers are no and there are long delays. You are looking at problems, not Me, and that steals your joy.

My precious one, I want you to stay with Me. Stay in My presence. I will be your joy and delight.

My Precious Treasure,

How glorious and magnificent are my works, and I marvel at them all. Do you realize that you are my magnificent and glorious creation? You are! I love you! I love you! I love you!

When you are rejected, neglected, hurt, and abused, come to Me. Let Me kiss and soothe the pain away. Stay with Me until you are healed. When you are well, I will go with you everywhere. I will be your buffer. When you are able to truly forgive, love, and pray for the offender with peace and joy, then you know you are healed. In the meantime, do not concern yourself with them, but know that this is a time for you to just sit and absorb My love, devotion, and healing arms. It is a time for Me to nurture and build you up. It is a time of repairing and soothing. It is a time of anointing you with My healing ointments.

The roadblocks and hindrances that come your way have been allowed by Me to bring you even closer to Me. I have a higher place to take you. I have so much more that I want to bless you with. How fast you come into this place of blessing depends on the amount of gratefulness and thankfulness you offer in the place you are in. You can receive all the joy and peace that you choose to receive from Me even in your circumstances. You can wildly dance with Me in thanksgiving and praise. You can lie down intoxicated in My love. My child, no one can take My love, peace, and joy from you. No one, no circumstance, and no demon from hell can separate you from My love. Dwell on this thought.

LOVE LETTERS TO MY QUEEN BRIDE

My Precious One,

I am always with you. You are never alone. I am more real than life itself. I am more real than any person. When you are forgotten, neglected, and abused, I am here, right here for you. You only need Me. Don't dwell on the hurt. Satan is alive and well. It is his fault that you were treated this way. Remember, there is a war going on. Satan would love for you to become bitter, depressed, and full of self pity. Don't give in to his tactics. Come to Me at the slightest sadness and let Me love on you. Stay with Me until you are filled to overflowing with My precious Spirit. There is nothing wrong with you. You are complete in Me. You are totally acceptable to Me. I delight in our friendship and bond of love. I love everything about you! You are an exciting fun person—delightful in every way!

You are never dull and boring. You are never "too bad" to be My friend. You are always interesting to talk to. I have all the time in the world for you. I am never too busy for you.

Relax in Me. Relax in My love. Be nice to yourself today. I am not giving you a "to do" list, but I want you to cling to me today so that I can meet all your social and emotional needs. I am your best friend! I love you!

My Precious One,

I know you are alone. I see what you face alone, but you are not alone. You have Me. I will always be your strongest supporter. Never mind if you are ignored, snubbed, chapped, disrespected, or even talked to ugly or abruptly. My love is powerful enough for you to be able to handle all of that. I love you so immensely, powerfully, deeply, passionately, and unconditionally that it will all be okay. You are My delight, My treasure, My prize, the apple of My eye, My queen, and My delight. I am obsessed over you and would be crucified all over again, just for you.

Enjoy Me as I enjoy you. Be enraptured with Me as I am with you. You are My magnificent, awesome queen. I treasure and cherish you. My heart swells with joy, passion, and devotion when I think of you.

When you go out in the world, know I am with you. I give you My Holy Spirit who will be your guide and comforter. He will not let you slip or fall. He will guide you into all truth. You will know the truth. You will hear My voice. You will feel My comfort. You will know when to speak and when to be quiet.

Don't worry and don't be afraid. Remember, perfect love casts out all fear. Love is easy. Love is the truth. I love you. I live in you. We are one.

Don't fear bad things to happen. Know I am your protector. Know that I will always love you and will be comforting you. I will always be your comforter.

My Precious One,

There is nothing and no one who can fully satisfy except Me. When you are absorbed in Me you find total peace, joy, and security. When you look anywhere else or to anyone else, you will become flat, depressed, without joy, peace and assurance. Things will make you happy. People will bring you love and joy. Enjoy all the good things that come to you, but only look to Me to fully satisfy. Then you will stay full and be overwhelmed with blessings.

When the enemy in others resists Me, My words, and My anointing, trust in Me. Pull into Me. I am your peace. I am your joy. When the enemy fires a bomb or causes interference, know I will cover, comfort, and protect you and the ones who love Me. Nothing can separate them or you from My love and peace—not even Satan's darts and bombs.

LOVE LETTERS TO MY QUEEN BRIDE

My Precious One,

I know you are hurting again. You are wise to acknowledge your pain and not try to stuff it. You are also wise to come to Me. The reason they are cold towards you is because they are cold towards Me. I live in you. I felt the rejection because we are bonded together. I wish they would love us, too. We can only pray for them. There are others who love us. We can fellowship with them and enjoy our time with them.

Be careful of self-pity. It is so easy to get into that when you are rejected. Also be careful of low self-worth. The other crippler is bitterness towards the ones who have rejected you. You must detach from all those wretched demons. Life is too abundant and there are so many other people who love you that you can enjoy.

You are spinning wheels in the mud again when you try to win the game of gaining their approval. You will actually make your situation worse if you are maneuvering all these plans to win their love. The only thing you can do is just love them. Maybe you need lots of distance from them in order to do this. Come to Me and let Me fill your love tank to overflowing and then you can really love them, not just play the "win approval" game. If you stay very close to Me, I will show you the difference. Using all your energy to try to win their love is a form of denying the real pain you are feeling because of the rejection. The truth is, they may reject you anyway. My child, come to Me. It is the only comforting way to go through life. Let Me fill your love tank with My love and keep you filled. I will do all the loving through you and you won't be left empty and all used up by trying to win others' love. I am love and I will never leave you or leave you feeling all used up.

My arms are outstretched to you right now. I want to hold you, comfort you, and love you. Will you let Me? I think you are wonderful! If you remember, I created you and what I make and create I do perfectly! You, My Love, are My precious and awesome creation. I think you are exquisite, marvelous—My masterpiece! You, My love, make Me want to shout, dance, and sing! You fully delight Me!

LOVE LETTERS TO MY QUEEN BRIDE

My Love,

I see your deep anger that borderlines on rage. It is O.K. to be really angry sometimes. I was too, at times. You know that if only My children would come to Me, let Me love them, and they obey Me they would be so much happier. When the people who are closest to you are away from Me you feel their pain and frustration. You hurt for them and feel sorry for them. As a human you also feel hurt because they haven't been to you the way you would have them to be.

My Queen, My Love, My precious sweetheart, it is time to detach from them. Let go of false guilt. They will sometimes try to dump this on you when you are in Me and in My will. Sometimes they want your life to revolve around them and they are not in Me and My will 100%. Don't accept the guilt they would try to ensnare you with. When they come into My will, they will be in harmony with you as long as you remain in Me.

Now, My precious love, come to Me. Let Me consume you with Myself—with joy, peace, love, truth, and contentment. Let go, detach from the world, and drink until you are intoxicated with my Holy Spirit. It is okay to let go of them. You can't fix them. You can't make them love Me or you. I created them to have a free will; to choose how much relationship they want from Me. You must let go of all control and maneuvering to make this happen.

My precious one, they have the same opportunity as you to come to Me, to drink from my cup of joy and fullness for their life. You become unhappy when you are focused on them and not Me. Their unhappiness is their choice. Don't allow them to pull you into their mediocre way of life, their "luke warmness" with Me. You will feel the persecution as they try to make you feel guilty. They want to be the center of their life and not Me. They may say you are not devoted to them, not loving enough, and even accuse you of not acting like a Christian should.

Come away with Me. Come into contentment with Me. You can't always please them. Even if you tried to, you would wind up in frustration, failure and confusion. I am the only one you can fully please and have true peace and fulfillment with. Stay with Me, My love. The more you stay with Me the better are the chances of them coming to Me.

Sometimes you feel the pain and aloneness of being separated from your loved ones. I feel the pain, too, but My love you can't do anything to make them come into My will. You can continue to pray for them and then let go. I promise you, I have heard and hear all your prayers for them.

Now refocus. Focus on Me, My Kingdom work, and My word. Be filled until overflowing with My Spirit until your joy and peace are overflowing. Stay close to Me. Take breaks with Me until you are renewed and refreshed for your next task. Please stay with Me. I won't disappoint you or let you down. Keep your eyes on Me. Keep your mind on Me. I love You!

LOVE LETTERS TO MY QUEEN BRIDE

My Fabulous Beautiful Awesome Bride,

I cherish and adore you. I am enraptured with you! Everything about you I made just right. Thank you so much for allowing Me to fill every part of your being.

Today I will empower you to forgive everyone. You have asked me to take over in your life and I will. I do not want you to suffer anymore. You have suffered much. The suffering you have endured has enlarged your capacity for My anointing. I fill you now with My glory. My glory is overshadowing your ego so that you are able to forgive.

When you are hurt it causes My Spirit in you to grieve. You are human. You are also filled with My glory, therefore I will not let the spirit of grief attach itself to you. This spirit brings with it bitterness, the inability to forgive, and causes you to stay stuck in suffering.

This is a new day and the brightness of My glory is consuming you now. You radiate with My light, love and anointing. You will live and be led by My glory.

I have so wonderfully made you in My image that I can't resist you. Because you are made in My image and I have breathed My breath into you, you can't resist Me. We are inseparable—you and Me, Me and you. We are one in My Spirit.

My Cherished Child,

I want you to see Me laughing. Yes, I laugh at Satan's schemes and ploys because I always win. I always prevail. Satan will never outwit Me or overpower Me. My promises to My beloved I will keep. You are My beloved. When you are afraid, hurt, distraught, and confused, know that I am with you and in you. See Me in control of your situation and laugh. I want you to have a light and joyful heart. I want to see you laughing at Satan's schemes because your heart is full of faith and joy knowing that I will deliver My promises and blessings to those who love and obey Me.

Rejoice, be glad, and even laugh as you see the wonderful and marvelous plan of escape I have for the multitudes that are lost and hurting. I am giving you and others My Spirit and My words to minister to them. My Spirit in you is one that bubbles up with joy and peace. At the slightest feeling of depression, anxiety, and unrest, come to Me and let Me pour into you My oil of joy and peace. Let Me move you from gloom and doom. I want to love you. I want to tell you how precious and wonderful you are to Me. I want to tell you about the wonderful plans I have for you. I want to tell you that I am taking care of all your prayer requests. Stop looking at the problem and look to Me. Don't think on and talk about how big your problem is but think on and talk about how wonderful, compassionate, and powerful I am.

I don't need your help in saving the world. I need for you to surrender to The Holy Spirit so I can reach a lost world, through you. I don't need for you to get your family and friends to obey Me. I need for you to submit and obey My Spirit so I can love them through you. You can never be someone else's Holy Spirit. They may never submit to Me but I can keep you filled with My peace, joy, and love even in the midst of their disobedience to Me.

You can cease your war with Satan because I have already won. What you do, and need to do is resist Satan and he will flee. You resist him when you praise and worship Me, when you minister My gifts with compassion and love, and when you listen and obey Me.

Again, I tell you. I love you deeply. When you are alone and Satan is raging, see yourself with your head on My chest and My arms around you. Experience and feel the tenderness that I have for you as My arms embrace you. The battle is Mine, the problem is Mine, and I win. I win in you and through you.

My Precious One,

You are so precious to Me. I know your heart. Your heart is full of mercy. I look for merciful hearts to pour out My mercy upon.

Sometimes you are frustrated and hurt with those who abuse My spiritual gifts and those who spiritually abuse you or those you love. Sometimes you are frustrated with those who don't believe My spiritual gifts are for today. They may try to persuade you or others not to believe My gifts are for today. Then in the midst of all your frustration you feel overwhelmed with the whole mess. Your emotions are valid. You don't have to apologize to Me. My Spirit inside you feels with you.

What is the answer? You must have a heart of mercy to all. You must have mercy. Feel your feelings and then have mercy. My last words on the cross were "Father, forgive them for they know not what they do." If they could believe they wouldn't be causing so many problems for themselves and others. You will be able to forgive them because My Spirit lives in you and will enable you to love and forgive them. I will grace you to do this. They need My love. Will you carry My love to them? Will you relax in My love so I can love them through you? I'm not asking you to do great and mighty feats for Me. I am asking you to relax in My love so that I can love through you.

LOVE LETTERS TO MY QUEEN BRIDE

Your greatest task is to soak in My love continuously. Place yourself in environments where you will be watered, fed, and fertilized. Surround yourself with people who will pour in My love to you. Seek to be loved in your quiet times with Me. You can't give what you don't have. Nobody wants a dried up sponge. You must soak in My love until it drips off you.

You and they need My love. When you and they are hurt and needy, there is the tendency to maintain control of your life and to make wrong choices and beliefs. But come to Me. Soak in My Love. Soak until your left hand doesn't know what your right hand is doing. You will love them. Love is the key. My agape love will flow through you, not just your human love.

Direction

FOR MY BELOVED

DIRECTION FOR MY BELOVED

My Love,

When you are in your "should and should not's," it is time to pull away from everyone and come to Me. When you need to feel confident of My directions and guidance come to Me. It is time to be quiet and very still until you are sure of the way to go.

An eagle senses the current of the wind before he flies, so that he goes with the current. So it is with you and My Spirit. It is so much easier for the eagle to fly with the current than against it. When life is rushing all around you and everything and every need may seem urgent and demanding, it is time to pause and check with My Spirit so that you are flowing with Me and letting Me carry you in My current of love, strength, energy, passion, compassion, and peace. Apart from Me you are useless. You may do more damage than good in your own self-efforts. I have a perfect design and plan for your life. I have a perfect design for your thought life and emotions each day. These thoughts and prayers will cause you to say and do My perfect will for you each day.

You are so loved. Let Me carry you, My beautiful strong eagle. We have so many skies to fly.

My Beautiful Bride,

Does it always seem like there are so many things that need to be accomplished and not enough time, energy, inspiration, sureness of direction, joy, peace, and love? I am here to tell you I am your Maker and Maintainer. There is enough inspiration, sureness of direction, time, energy, joy, love, and peace with Me. I am with you and in you all the time. I told you we are one. I am the Vine and you are the Branch. My will is for you to live in My glory. You live in My glory by surrendering your whole self every minute to Me. You live in My glory by thanking, praising, worshiping Me, listening to Me and letting Me speak and act through you continuously.

DIRECTION FOR MY BELOVED

My Precious One,

I delight in your joy and peace in Me! I am so glad that you desire to spend quality time with Me. Not just for My sake, but because I see what a difference it makes in your life.

You finally realize what really makes you content!

You are so precious to Me! Precious! My angels are with you to help you all throughout your days and nights. You are My precious one. I am The King—The #1 Man in Authority. I am The Royal Highness. You are My Royal Child. You are My Bride, My Queen. Everyone will know who you are in My Kingdom. You have royal blood flowing through your veins because I bought you with My life and you are immersed in the blood I shed for you on the cross. I am The King of Kings and Lord of Lords—The Most High God and you are by My side. I have given you power to rule and reign in My authority because of My finished work on the cross. This also has gained for you My royal Power of Attorney. Be kind. I want you to be loving, respectful, and humble. Never be arrogant, haughty, or rude. Be ready to wash feet and to sit at feet. Be ready to love and listen. Be willing to speak the words that I will put in your mouth. Be loved. Receive My love. Soak in My love. You must wait on Me. Wait on Me. I will give you what you need.

As a flower soaks up sun and water, so must you take much time to soak up My love and words to you. The more you soak up the more you will be able to give out. I want you to be dripping with My love.

When you study My word, study it to find My love for you. My kingdom comes when you soak up so much love that when you minister, your right hand won't know what your left hand is doing. I want you so caught up in My love that all you see is Me in all situations.

My Treasured One,

I love you! My delight is in you! I marvel at My creation! My Spirit in you is glorious, divine, and I am awed!

My love, you have understood! It is not about doing more, being more, getting it better, being better or getting more. It is all about loving and being loved. As you drink in My love, My love flows out to others. As you absorb My mercy, My tenderness, and My devotion to you, you are able to pour out mercy, tenderness and devotion to others. So, My bride, My exquisite treasure, keep on keeping on. Keep absorbing My love and devotion to you and relaxing in My love.

Dear One,

Open up your heart. Let go and surrender. Don't try to figure anything out. Trust Me. I will give you the perfect words. Any problem is not your problem. It is My problem. I live in you. Relax. Come and lay your head on My heart. Let Me love you. Let Me hold you and tell you everything is going to be all right.

When you are weak, then I can be strong in you. When you are unable, I am able. When you don't know the way, remember, I am The Way. Lose yourself in worship and then wait on Me to speak to you. Listen to Me speak to you and then lose yourself in praise and worship.

Don't neglect the needs of your family. Don't neglect your own need to rest and delight in Me. I am with you and in you. I am love and life. I delight in you. I will take care of you and meet all your needs.

DIRECTION FOR MY BELOVED

My Love,

It is very hard to cut a potato with a dull knife. It is very difficult to accomplish My work without much prayer. Keep in communion with Me constantly in order to do My work with ease. It will be like having a sharp knife to cut a potato.

Use the correct tool when you are doing My work. You wouldn't use pliers to get out a splinter, but tweezers. Listen very carefully to Me to know what tool to use and when. Also, you may have a correct tool for a job, but there may be a more efficient one. A food processor instead of a knife would be a quicker way to get more accomplished. So it is with the gifts of My Spirit.

You will need to listen carefully to know which gift of My Spirit to use in what circumstance. I will supply what gift you need to do My work as you go. Stay close to Me. I am always with you. You will grow in discernment as you obey Me. The more you obey, the more discernment you will receive.

What I desire most is that you enjoy Me and rest in Me. I am delighted with you and love your delight in Me. My yoke fits easily and My burdens are light. When you are heavily burdened know that it is not My yoke you are carrying. Come to Me and rest with Me. I will lift your burden and give you My peace.

As you delight and rest in Me, I will be working through you with My gifts so that your right hand will not know what your left hand is doing. I am here to simplify your life. I truly have come that you might have life and have it more abundantly. Cast all your care—all—upon Me, for I care for you deeply. I am concerned about every detail of your life. Ask Me and expect Me to remove duties that wear you out. I want to free you so that you can be about My work.

I don't want so much for you to do things for Me, but for you to allow Me to work through you, then you can accomplish what I have in mind. This will free you of the responsibility. You are never responsible for results, just obedience to yield and surrender to My Spirit.

You will always stumble and lose your way by focusing first on pleasing man. You desire love and affirmation. As you seek only to please Me, you will receive much love and affirmation—not only by Me, but by men also. Even by pleasing Me, there will be pain and hurt from others, but there will always be Me to hold, love, affirm, and lift you back up quickly.

DIRECTION FOR MY BELOVED

My Child,

Once you have entered into My kingdom and are quiet and content before Me, look around. I will show you those who are hurting, in sorrow, and bound up. I will show you where they are hurting and bound up. Be quiet and listen to Me as I use you to minister to them. Don't give them your advice; give them only what I speak through you. I will give you words of knowledge, prophetic words, and prophetic songs. You will see miracles I will work right before your eyes.

Before you begin ministering to others, come first to Me with your pain. I will help you to identify the source. I will heal you and mend your broken heart. You must be compassionate first with yourself so that I can heal you. Then go in compassion towards others, remembering I will work through you.

As you move in My plans, I will take care of the things that concern you. They will be taken care of as you let go and move forward with Me. Don't be afraid or discontented. I will be with you. I will never ever leave you. I will instruct you in the way you are to go.

My Child,

I am more interested in your being than in your doing. There will always be the cares of this world and things that need to be done. I am asking you to drop what keeps you from walking in My presence and keeps robbing your joy in Me.

Yesterday's anointing won't work for today. Each day you need a new anointing. Seek Me first, above all, and you will receive what you need.

You are just as much under My anointing when I speak with a small still voice and you feel no emotion as when I speak with a loud voice and you feel very emotional. My anointing is on you when you are listening to Me and obeying Me. Many times I am calling you to speak a prophetic word or word of knowledge, but you are fearful, not listening to Me, or don't think you are holy or emotional enough. Just as you received eternal life only by believing, you can step out in my gifting simply by believing. You didn't have to be "good" enough to be saved. Neither do I require you to be "good" enough to speak out with My words.

Often fear holds you back, but I am asking you to step out in My perfect love and power. My perfect love casts out all fear. I am asking you to move in compassion and love to hurting people. I will give you my words for their healing, comfort, and encouragement.

DIRECTION FOR MY BELOVED

My Child,

Don't beat on hearts with closed doors. Don't beg tight-fisted hands to open. Stop prying, pleading and begging. Never criticize or scold. Join My love song and dance to My heartbeat. Let Me lead you. Rejoice with those who rejoice. Dance with those who will dance. Love with those who will love. I will show you the open doors, the open hands and hearts. Love and be loved. I love you.

LOVE LETTERS TO MY QUEEN BRIDE

My Precious Queen,

You are allowing Me to fill your heart with even more compassion. You are listening and obeying Me more. I am calling you now to even have compassion for the world—even those you don't know. I will use you in a powerful way to minister to more people on a larger scale and a more powerful way than you have experienced at this point.

Just as you have stayed linked to Me, continue to do that. Ask Me for more compassion for the world and to expand your focus and vision. Don't get anxious or run ahead of Me, but also stay focused on ministering to the world. Don't ignore your ministry to your family and smaller circles. Be conscientious, attentive, and thorough. I would never call you to a world ministry to take away your commitment to your family and friends.

Pay attention to your health. Get the exercise you need. Eat the correct foods and the right amount. Eliminate unnecessary activities that create stress in your life. Take My words seriously. Your health is important for the work I have planned for you.

You will love what I have planned for you! I am taking you to a higher level. It is a place of more joy, peace, and fulfillment than you have ever known!

Rest in My love, relax in My embrace, jump for joy at what I have in store for you!

My Precious One,

I have you safe in My heavenly cocoon. It is safe, soft, and warm. I am fully nurturing you until you are ready to break out and fly. My angels guard the cocoon day and night so that intruders cannot puncture the cocoon.

Don't worry. There will be no flying assignment until you are fully developed and strong.

You don't have to worry about being "on time" with the flying assignment I have for you. If you stay close to Me and in Me, you will mature and be ready. You will know beyond a doubt when it is time to break out and fly. I love you so much! I will always be your loving Daddy.

My Royal Child,

My peace and presence are on you. I wash you clean with My blood. The praise and worship you offer Me brings healing to your soul. You are strengthened through My words. Your prayers for those among you have been heard. I will lead, guide, and direct you. Listen to Me, believe Me, and rest in My love.

My Precious One,

I am with you and in you. I will guide you exactly in the paths you should go. My Holy Spirit in you is powerful, loving, and full of mercy. I love you. I will not let you fail. You can trust Me. Nothing can separate you from My love.

My Son sits at my right hand constantly interceding on your behalf and for those who belong to Me. When you are weary with intercession, know that you can release those you love and care for into My care.

My Precious One,

Yes, you are precious and priceless to Me. I gave My very life for you! I will not hurt you or harm you. Don't be afraid of Me. Don't be afraid to trust Me. I will only lead you in the right way. I will hold you close. I will keep a tight grip on you. I will keep you next to My heart, always encouraging, affirming, and comforting you. I will do nothing but good for you. I will comfort and coax you in My way without criticizing, complaining, and condemning you. I am "The King" and I am a gentleman. I am "The Gentleman" of all gentlemen.

When you are in the way of danger, I will scoop you up like a giant eagle and secure you safely under My wing. I will safely place you where it will be best for you. I know the desires of your heart. I put those desires in you. I will lead you beside the still waters and green pastures. You will feed in safety. I will sing over you. I will be glorified through you!

I am going to use you in a huge way to further and enhance My Kingdom here on earth. All your thoughts, emotions, words, and actions are powerful for pulling down strongholds. I will put you in the right place at the right time, and you will respond to My love exactly right. Never fear, I am always near. Never fear, I am here—here in you. Satan trembles when you wake in the morning. Satan is terrified of you! Even though he roars sometimes, he is just a mouse with a megaphone. He is like a roach when the light is turned on—he flees to get back in the dark. My light shines brightly in you. You will see him running as you hear his criticism, whining, and complaining. Keep praising, worshiping, and drawing close to Me and watch him flee.

I love to cuddle up and draw you close to Me. I love holding you in My arms. I love encouraging, affirming, and comforting you. I love how you love Me! You are so precious to Me. I never tire of you. I always love having you near.

I am for you—never against you. I am all about joy, peace, and love. I am all about laughter, beauty, and light. I am all about life. I am your life.

My Cherished Child, My Adored Bride,

I love you deeply. Words cannot describe the depth of love that I have for you. I would go to the cross all over again for you if that were necessary.

What do you think on all day—what you need to do, should do or shouldn't do? What I want you to think on all day is My love for you. I am pouring My love on you now. I am soaking and drenching you in My love. You have been through the fire and you are weak. But remember that I have told you that in your weakness I can be strong in you. You are right where you need to be. Don't focus on accomplishing great and mighty things for Me. Focus on relaxing in My love. Let Me hold and rock you now. You are My love—My precious one I love. As you are absorbed in My love then I can accomplish great and mighty things through you.

Think on My forgiveness. Dwell on My forgiveness and grace at all times. Just as the father took back the prodigal son, so I put a ring on your finger, call for the fatted calf, and give a party to celebrate. You can't enjoy the celebration if you are hung up on what you need to do next or what you did that was wrong. The father wanted the son to enjoy Him and enjoy His love.

The son was so grateful that the father took him back. He was overcome by His love.

Those in your life that are straying and want your love and acceptance—do you take them back? Do you love and embrace and celebrate with them just where they are? I have made you weak for a purpose—to love, forgive, embrace, and celebrate with them.

Stay focused on My love and forgiveness. Apart from Me you can do nothing. It is only in My embrace, and in My celebration time of your return to Me that you can forgive and celebrate with others.

You never have to be "good enough" to receive My love and My forgiveness. My bride, My friend, My child, think on My forgiveness and My love daily, hourly, moment by moment. This is My great assignment, the great work I have called you to.

My Precious One,

I am here for you! You have been seeking and searching. I am here to give 100% of Myself to you—not part of Me, not a little of Me, and not Me on the run. I am so glad you realize today that you don't have to be good or holy enough to come to Me. I have noticed when you enjoyed Me working through you. I love being with you! I love your sticking with Me.

You often forget to come to Me first. You look for this or that or people to satisfy. I'm not telling you this to scold you or control you, but to remind you that complete satisfaction is found only in total surrender to Me.

When you sit down with Me and wait on Me to talk to you, you are in a position where you can hear Me the best. To the degree that you listen to Me and trust Me is to the degree of how I can help you the most and how we can best work together.

I will tell you who, what, when, and how. In the army, it is the general who discusses the best plan of action with those under his command. I have called you into My army. I am The General! Our mission is love. We win each battle with love. We accomplish each goal with love. You must have your love tank full before you set out on any assignment. I am the only one who can fill your love tank completely full. Each day come to Me early before you start your day. Allow Me time to fill you to overflowing with My love. Reading scripture is great. Worshiping Me is awesome. Intercessory prayer, repentance and forgiveness prayers are super. But My precious one, will you then be quiet and let Me just love you? Will you let Me just talk to you and tell you how much I love and adore you and how I deeply appreciate your friendship and devotion to Me. You don't have to be afraid of Me. I won't give you an assignment that you can't handle. I won't give you a life of drudgery and depression. It is only when you take control that you feel whipped, unfulfilled and unloved.

LOVE LETTERS TO MY QUEEN BRIDE

Precious One,

Do you know how much I love you? Do you feel My love towards you and in you? Only when you begin to assess it, will I require of you an assignment. If you find My assignment too difficult then go back to the place where you can receive My love the most. Are you feeling drenched in My love? When you are at this place then we can move forward. I won't push, force, or condemn you if you are not ready. I will know you only need more soaking in My love. This is how you will know that you have rested in My arms of love long enough. Think of the persons or person in your life that you find it the hardest to remain holy with? Is this an impossible order? Alone it is impossible but with Me nothing is impossible. Is there anything too difficult for Me? I will keep you holy. I in you will carry this assignment to completion.

Live with Me. Breathe with Me. I am in you and with you constantly, helping and loving you! Don't think about the person or the situations that you find difficult. Think about Me and My love. Let Me love you. Let Me love you more and more. Come to Me. Sing and dance with Me. Celebrate My love continuously. You can do that best when you praise and worship Me. As you praise and worship Me in a continuous way we remain locked in a powerhouse of love. No man or situation can break our bond or stop My love from going forth from you.

DIRECTION FOR MY BELOVED

Dear Beloved,

You are so intent on pleasing Me with your words and wanting "to do" the right and perfect thing for Me. It makes Me happy that you are intent on pleasing Me perfectly. I have something better for you and that will please Me more than anything you can "do" for Me. I just want you to be still with Me. Let Me talk to you. I already know ALL the things you are concerned about and all your requests for others and yourself. I will take care of all of that perfectly. I know you think or wonder sometimes if I heard you because "the answers" you requested are a long time in coming. You are forgetting that I know what is best for you, even better than you know yourself at times. If you would sit down, be still, be quiet, and just let Me love you, things will become a lot clearer to you. Seek Me first, not My will, not what you want, just Me. I want to love you and I want you to love Me. I will take care of everything. When Moses had the Egyptians on his heels and all his people on his heels, he didn't try to figure out a construction plan and hire engineers to get the Red Sea parted. He kept his eyes on Me. Remember the verse "I will keep him in perfect peace whose mind is stayed on Me."

Come My Precious One,

Drop your cares, concerns, worries, dread, and burdens. Come fly high with Me. See, I am doing a new thing. Drop your old caterpillar lifestyle and fly the skies that I have predestined for you. Now that you are a butterfly, what you did when you were a caterpillar just won't work.

I am the sun and this is a new day. Come, drink from the honeycomb of worship and praise. Feast on My sweet nectar, My precious promises to you. You are My eagle, fly over the storm. Fly high away from all cares and problems, knowing I am the wind beneath your wings.

What worked yesterday won't work for today. Why?—because I want you to come to Me each day for a fresh anointing. I am not McDonald's where you drive through for a quick fix. You must get still and quiet. There are good things you are doing that you must drop to make way for the best things I would have you to do. As you wait and worship before Me daily, I will pour on you all My love and let you see in the Spirit realm. As My glory is poured upon you, it will be Me doing and speaking through you.

My precious one, I am here now. My glory rests upon you. You are saturated in Me and My love. There are those around you who are waiting to hear Me speak, dance, and sing through you. Open the precious lips that I formed and fashioned and let Me shower My blessings on My children who surround you. I want to bless, comfort and encourage My precious children. Speak forth My healing words to them.

My Precious One,

Release all control in your life and just let Me love through you. Always minister in My anointing. The key to effective ministry is to listen and love and love and listen.

The key to intimacy with Me is to listen and love and love and listen. This will always save you from burn out and mistakes. Come to Me. Stay with Me. I will tell you where to go, what to do, how long to stay, and when to move on.

Remember, I am your healer, your lover, and your Savior. You are the vessel that I choose to work through. I will never put more on you than you can handle. Accept your limitations. Trust, rest, rely, and lean on Me, and then I will be able to work through you. I love you. I love you! I am with you, in you, and will never ever leave you!

My Precious One,

Oh, My child, I am so pleased with you and your obedience. Because you yield to Me, I will pour out through you even more of My power and gifting. Blessings upon blessings will be given to you as My pouring goes on. Your understanding of Me and My way is becoming clearer and clearer. You know that true joy and peace are in Me and My ways. Because of your obedience, I have given you discernment. My love in you will direct you in every circumstance. Lean not on your own understanding. Look to Me and what My Father is doing in every circumstance and do that. Keep your eyes and heart on Me and you will know. I will not fail you. I love you deeply. You are never responsible for the outcome, only for yielding to Me. Lean on Me and rest in Me. I will lead you through because I love you and you are Mine. You will always be Mine.

Allow Me to do and give to you. Those who ask the most of Me and allow Me to do and give to them understand My love for them the most. They are also the ones willing to yield to Me the most. Mary was a good example of this. Mary gave her time and attention to Me and let Martha cook. Mary was totally absorbed with Me. (Luke 10:38-42)

My Precious Child,

My precious one, I am pleased with you. Your worship is very pleasing to Me. I am The Way, The Truth, and The Life. When you can't find the way or if you are in the dark, hold My hand. I am already holding you. Ask Me for help. I will give you light. I will give you just enough light for what you need. I repeat: I am The Way, The Truth, and The Life.

You don't have to be good enough to come to Me. Come to Me just as you are. I forgive you. Buckets and buckets of mercy and love are raining on you. Buckets and buckets of love are drenching all over you.

DIRECTION FOR MY BELOVED

My Devoted One,

I see how sometimes you are so very fearful. You feel sometimes that I won't protect you. You acknowledge your sinfulness and ask for forgiveness. Sometimes you think that I won't keep you covered and bless you. None of My children, except Jesus, are perfect. They all sin and are disobedient. I still love them deeply and I protect and bless them when they turn to Me with a repentant heart. I will do the same for you. You don't have to earn My protection and care. I am a loving parent. You don't have to be Daddy's perfect performer in order for Me to lavish you with love and care. Your Daddy loves you when you are very bad. Your Daddy loves you all the time, good or bad. Your Daddy will love you no matter what. I just know you will be happier when you listen to Me and obey. I want to take you on special adventures, trips, and little excursions, just the two of us, where I can lavish you with My love and care. I love to do this with you, and for you.

Don't worry about a thing. Trust Me. Trust Me to be a good Daddy to you. I will, when I feel it is necessary, even keep your mistakes and failings hidden from those who would condemn you.

Think of a child whom you love dearly. Think about the great lengths you would go through to protect, nurture, and care for them. I love you even more and will do even more for you! Trust Me! Believe!

Your sin is not trusting Me and believing Me. Yes, I will even help you with the trusting and believing.

Thank You, Lord

Thank You, Lord

Dear God, my sweet Lord, I thank, praise and worship You! I adore Your Holy Name! I exalt You! You are awesome, fabulous, amazing, all powerful, mighty, great, marvelous, and wonderful beyond words!

My wonderful, merciful, gentle and sweet Lord, I cherish, treasure, and bless Your Holy Name. You are splendid, spectacular and altogether lovely. You are wonderful beyond words—irresistible! You are so worthy to be thanked, praised, worshiped and adored. Holy, holy, holy are You, Lord. I revere and honor You with all my heart. I thank, praise and worship You with all my heart, soul, mind, and strength. You are all that I need, all that I want, and worthy of all my praise.

You are my Great Comforter, Counselor, Protector, Provider, Healer, and Keeper. I give You all of me. Please come in and completely take over in my life. Thank You for being such an unconditionally Loving Daddy, Pastor, Best Friend and Spouse. Thank You that You let me be a Branch of Your very self, The Vine! Please forgive me of all my sin. Thank You! Thank You that You let Your Son die for all my sin and shame that I might be able to live abundantly in Your kingdom here on earth and through eternity with You in heaven! I bless You. I praise You. I thank and adore You. You are awesome, I exalt You!

Abba Father; precious Daddy God, I thank You for Your blessings and protection. Continue to fully bless, protect, and control me. Please fully bless, protect, and control my family, friends, and all believers everywhere. Let Your kingdom come and Your will be done on earth as it is in heaven. I love You!

Thank You, Lord

Dear God, my sweet Lord, I thank, praise and worship You! I adore Your Holy Name! I exalt You! You are awesome, fabulous, amazing, all powerful, mighty, great, marvelous, and wonderful beyond words!

My wonderful, merciful, gentle and sweet Lord, I cherish, treasure, and bless Your Holy Name. You are splendid, spectacular and altogether lovely. You are wonderful beyond words—irresistible! You are so worthy to be thanked, praised, worshiped and adored. Holy, holy, holy are You, Lord. I revere and honor You with all my heart. I thank, praise and worship You with all my heart, soul, mind, and strength. You are all that I need, all that I want, and worthy of all my praise.

You are my Great Comforter, Counselor, Protector, Provider, Healer, and Keeper. I give You all of me. Please come in and completely take over in my life. Thank You for being such an unconditionally Loving Daddy, Pastor, Best Friend and Spouse. Thank You that You let me be a Branch of Your very self, The Vine! Please forgive me of all my sin. Thank You! Thank You that You let Your Son die for all my sin and shame that I might be able to live abundantly in Your kingdom here on earth and through eternity with You in heaven! I bless You. I praise You. I thank and adore You. You are awesome, I exalt You!

Abba Father; precious Daddy God, I thank You for Your blessings and protection. Continue to fully bless, protect, and control me. Please fully bless, protect, and control my family, friends, and all believers everywhere. Let Your kingdom come and Your will be done on earth as it is in heaven. I love You!

To order more from
Beth C. Walker

Visit
www.queenbride.com
or
www.bethcwalker.com

About the Author

Beth Walker has been married to her husband Ben for over 40 years. She is the mother of three adult children and seven grandchildren that she adores.

After raising her children she founded a Christian counseling center where she served as director and counselor for sixteen years. She also founded and directed in her home town Drug Free Clubs for high risk youth at 23 sites. For over eleven years she has led an interdenominational worship group. She also has served as a Christian speaker, Sunday school teacher, and Eucharistic minister.

Among the various organizations that she has served as volunteer include the Board of the Montgomery Mental Health Association for twelve years and the Montgomery Board of Women's Aglow International.

She is quick to say only through the help of the Holy Spirit was she able to do anything and will be able to do anything in the future. Her passion is Christ. She says, soaking in worship and then listening to Him, after knowing His word is the only way to go.

(Left to right) Gracie Walker, Anne McKinley Walker, Lilly Turner, Beth Walker, June Turner, Melanie Beth Cawthon, Sarah Cawthon

Made in the USA
Lexington, KY
03 January 2016